WHISPERS WITHIN

THE POWER OF WOMEN'S INTUITION

JULIE FAIRHURST

ROCK STAR PUBLISHING

WHISPERS WITHIN
THE POWER OF WOMEN'S INTUITION
Compiled by Julie Fairhurst

The authors of this book do not dispense medical advice or prescribe the use of any
technique as a form of treatment for physical, emotional, or medical problems without a
physician's advice, either directly or indirectly. The authors intend to provide general
information to individuals taking positive steps in their lives for emotional and spiritual
well-being. If you use any information in this book for yourself, which is your
constitutional right, the authors and the publishers assume no responsibility for your
actions.

At times, some readers may be triggered by a women's story. Should you need to speak
with someone, there are many crisis lines, counselors, and doctors that you can reach
out to. Find someone who can lend a kind ear to listen to you. That can be a friend,
parent, spouse, or anyone you trust. Your local community services may have telephone
numbers to assist you.

CONTENTS

"The only real valuable thing is intuition."
Albert Einstein

INTRODUCTION

Welcome to "Whispers Within The Power of Women's Intuition," a collaborative creation by women from diverse backgrounds who unite to share their personal and enlightening encounters with intuition.

This book delves into and celebrates the gentle inner voice present in every woman, offering guidance on acknowledging, comprehending, and utilizing the force of intuition. It is a tribute to the quiet yet potent influence within each of us.

Intuition is often likened to a gut instinct, an inexplicable sense of knowing, or a deep-seated instinctual feeling. It surpasses mere guess-work. While inherent in all individuals, women, in particular, are renowned for their acute intuitive power, aiding them in crucial decision-making across personal and professional domains.

Through personal anecdotes, reflection, and practical advice, the authors of this book delve deep into the essence of intuition. They share moments where intuition guided crucial decisions and the lessons learned from ignoring it.

"Whispers Within" aims to empower you to trust your inner voice, revealing that intuition is mystical and practical.

Intuition connects us with our inner selves, enhancing empathy, guiding choices, and protecting us. By embracing these whispers, we align with authenticity and live more fully. The stories invite reflection on personal experiences with intuition, guiding you to deepen your connection to this inner resource. Whether a skeptic or intuitive, "Whispers Within" offers transformative insights for all.

"Whispers Within" is more than a book; it's an opportunity to delve into your inner world and unlock the profound potential of intuition, a timeless force that has guided women through the ages. Embrace this innate gift, heed your inner voice, and navigate life's complexities with poise and certainty.

Let this book be your companion on a journey of self-discovery, helping you distinguish intuition from everyday noise and harness its power for personal growth and fulfillment.

Julie Fairhurst

"That what I have is not women's intuition but a finely honed copper's instinct for when things aren't right."
Val McDermid

MY FRIEND
INTUITION

Her name is Intuition, and she is a good friend of mine.
Let me tell you quickly about her.

We meet often and chat about gut feelings and raw situations.
She is a non-censored, non-judgmental zone.

She is loud, confident, and doesn't like being told.
She is never late and always on time.
Has my back at the drop of a dime.

She often shows up unannounced, walking right into the circle or
crowd without skipping a beat. She loves to gossip but hates drama,
takes great pride in investing in conversations, and eagerly gives me
the details of all that we meet.

She can be bossy, oh so bossy, when she wants to leave.
She has zero issues voicing her dislikes or
how something made her feel.

She is fun and dances when her interest is peaked.
She tends to be softer and calm with her approach when she finds
something that sparks her inner peace.

Like a creative artist in the middle of a masterpiece. Calculated and
observant.
She is quick and witty. She is fast to recalculate routes when we avoid
certain streets.

She is a beautiful, heart-stopping, gut-clenching know-it-all!

As wild and unhinged as she may sound,
she is the reason for why I am around.
I wouldn't want her to be any other way!

Rhonda Funk

"Enlightenment is at the source of everything. From it, flows our Intuition and our creative energy.

It is the delta of the human spirit $\sim$ what we innately seek to return to, as we find ourselves lost in this world."
Kim Chestney

PART 1

THE POWER OF WOMEN'S INTUITION

1

UNDERSTANDING INTUITION—WHAT IT IS AND WHAT IT IS NOT

Intuition, an elusive concept often shrouded in mystery, has been described in various ways—as a gut feeling, a sixth sense, or an inexplicable knowing. It's an inherent part of human nature, yet it remains one of the least understood aspects of our consciousness. To harness its power effectively, we must first explain intuition and understand what it is and what it is not.

Intuition is not a magical phenomenon, or a mystical gift bestowed upon a select few. It's not a random stroke of luck or a divine whisper in the ear. Rather, it's an innate ability that we all possess, a subtle form of knowledge that comes from within. It's our subconscious mind processing information faster than our conscious mind can keep up with.

When we talk about having a 'gut feeling,' it's not just a figure of speech. There's a scientific basis for this phrase. Our gut or nervous system is often called our 'second brain.' It communicates with our primary brain via the nerve, sending signals about our internal state. This 'gut-brain' communication can manifest as feelings of unease or comfort, which we interpret as intuitive signals.

Understanding intuition is not about debunking its mystery but rather about acknowledging its roots in our subconscious mind and physiological responses. By doing so, we can learn to trust our intuition more, using it as a tool for decision-making and problem-solving. We can learn to differentiate between irrational fears and genuine intuitive warnings, between wishful thinking and intuitive guidance.

Understanding intuition doesn't diminish its power; it enhances it. By understanding the science behind our 'sixth sense,' we can harness its power more effectively, using it to navigate our lives more confidently and clearly. So the next time you get a 'gut feeling,' don't dismiss it as mere superstition. Recognize it as your intuition speaking to you, a powerful ally in your journey through life.

What Intuition Is

Intuition, an inherent part of human cognition, is often associated with gut feelings or sixth sense. It is a natural and essential function that plays a pivotal role in how we perceive, understand, and react to the world around us. This automatic, instantaneous process equips us with the ability to know something directly without the need for analytic reasoning.

This fascinating cognitive process bridges the gap between our mind's conscious and nonconscious parts. It enables us to make decisions, form judgments, and solve problems quickly and efficiently, often without us even realizing it. It's like having an internal compass guiding us through life, helping us navigate complex situations easily and confidently.

Intuition: The Unseen Power Within

Intuition, often misunderstood as a mystical ability to predict the future or a form of psychic prowess, is, in fact, a more grounded and accessible mental resource. It is not about peering into a crystal ball but rather about tapping into the vast reservoir of information, experiences, and patterns stored in our subconscious mind.

Our subconscious mind is like a vast library filled with every piece of information we've ever encountered, every experience we've had, and every pattern we've noticed. It's a treasure trove of knowledge we often overlook in our daily lives. But when we tap into this resource, we can make connections between seemingly unrelated facts and figures and come up with insights that logical thinking might overlook.

Intuition is about making these connections. It's about seeing the patterns others might miss, drawing on our past experiences to make sense of the present, and using all the information at our disposal to make informed decisions. It's about trusting our gut feelings, even when they seem to contradict the facts and figures in front of us.

So next time you're faced with a difficult decision, don't just rely on logic and reason. Tap into your intuition. Trust your gut. You might be surprised at the insights you uncover.

While intuition is a natural function, it can be honed and improved with practice. We can enhance our intuitive abilities by paying attention to our inner voice, trusting our instincts, and not overthinking. In a world that's increasingly reliant on data and analytics, intuition serves as a reminder of the power and potential of the human mind.

So, trust your intuition the next time you find yourself at a crossroads, unsure of which path to take. It's a natural human function, an essential part of our cognition, and a powerful tool that can help us make better decisions, solve problems more effectively, and lead a more fulfilling life.

A Source of Quick Insight: The Power of Intuition

In an age where data-driven decision-making is the gold standard, intuition is a seemingly mystical force that often gets overlooked. It's an elusive concept, often dismissed as irrational or unscientific. Yet, it's a cognitive process that we all possess and use, often without even realizing it.

Intuition arises as a response to situations where there is insufficient information or no apparent logical answer. It's the brain drawing on past experiences, emotions, and environmental cues to make a decision quickly and effectively. It's the mental equivalent of a seasoned firefighter who can sense danger before it's visible or a mother who instinctively knows when her child is in distress.

While it may seem like intuition is a spontaneous process, it's actually a result of our brains rapidly processing information from our past experiences and our present environment. Our brains constantly absorb information, even when we're unaware of it. This information forms a vast database of knowledge that our intuition can draw upon in times of need.

So, how can we harness the power of intuition?

The first step is to acknowledge its value. While data and logic should form the basis of our decision-making process, intuition can provide valuable insight when these resources are limited or unclear. It's about striking a balance between the rational and the intuitive and understanding that both have their place in our cognitive toolkit.

Next, we need to cultivate our intuition. This involves becoming more attuned to our feelings and emotions and learning to trust our gut instincts. It also means paying attention to the world and being open to new experiences that can enrich our internal knowledge database.

Finally, we need to practice using our intuition. Like any skill, it becomes stronger with use. This means making decisions based on our gut feelings and then reflecting on the outcomes. Over time, we'll become more confident in our intuitive abilities and better able to use them to our advantage.

Intuition is a powerful tool that can provide quick insight into situations lacking logic and information. By acknowledging its value, cultivating it, and practicing its use, we can enhance our decision-making abilities and navigate the world more confidently and effectively.

An Emotional GPS: The Power of Intuition

Intuition, often perceived as a mysterious inner voice, has long been a topic of intrigue and speculation. It's like an internal compass, gently nudging us towards decisions and actions that may not always align with conventional logic yet resonate deeply with our core values and needs.

The Subtle Nudge

Intuition is subtle yet powerful. It's not a loud, demanding voice but a soft whisper that guides us when we're at a crossroads, unsure of which path to take. It's that inexplicable feeling that something is right or wrong, even when we can't quite put our finger on why.

A Deep Connection

At its core, intuition is deeply connected to our values and needs. It's an internal barometer measuring the alignment between our actions and deepest beliefs. We feel a sense of peace and rightness when we make decisions that align with our values. Conversely, when we go against our intuition, we often experience unease and discomfort.

Logic vs Intuition

While logic is based on facts and evidence, intuition operates on a different plane. It transcends the boundaries of logical reasoning and ventures into the realm of the subconscious. It's not irrational, but rather non-rational. It doesn't dismiss logic but complements it, providing a holistic approach to decision-making.

Embracing the Power of Intuition

Recognizing and embracing the power of intuition can be transformative. It's about trusting ourselves, our feelings, and our ability to make the right decisions. It's about tuning into our inner compass and allowing it to guide us on our journey.

So, the next time you feel that gentle nudge, don't dismiss it. Listen to it. Trust it. It's your emotional GPS, guiding you towards decisions and actions that align with your deepest values and needs.

What Intuition Is Not

Unraveling the Mysteries of Intuition

Intuition, a term often used in casual conversation and professional discourse, is frequently misunderstood. It's a concept that has been mystified, romanticized, and sometimes oversimplified. One common misconception is that intuition is simply an emotional reaction. However, this couldn't be further from the truth.

While it's true that intuition can involve emotions, it's crucial to understand that it is not purely an emotional reaction. This understanding is a significant step towards demystifying the concept of intuition and appreciating its complexity.

Intuition is a rapid, unconscious process incorporating insights from various mental processes. Emotions are indeed a part of this mix, but they are not the sole contributors. Intuition is a sophisticated cognitive function that draws on past experiences, subconscious observations, and even our innate ability to recognize patterns.

So, the next time you attribute a decision or insight to your 'intuition,' remember that there's more to it than just an emotional response. You're tapping into a complex cognitive process that's working behind the scenes, integrating information from various mental processes to guide your decisions and actions.

Understanding intuition in this light gives us a greater appreciation for our cognitive abilities and helps us better use our intuitive insights in both personal and professional contexts.

Not Infallible: The Role of Intuition in Decision-Making

In the realm of decision-making, intuition often holds a revered place. It's that gut feeling, that inner voice that nudges us towards a particular direction. However, it's crucial to understand that intuition is not always right. It's a cognitive process that can influence biases, past experiences, and emotional scars.

While powerful, intuition is not infallible. It's akin to a compass in a dense forest—it can guide you but can't map out the entire terrain. It's a tool, a piece of the puzzle, not the entire picture. It's important to recognize that intuition should be one of many tools in decision-making, not the only one.

Biases, both conscious and unconscious, can color our intuition. These biases can stem from our upbringing, cultural background, or personal experiences. They can skew our intuitive responses, leading us astray. For instance, if we've had negative experiences with a particular group of people, our intuition might unfairly warn us against interacting with them. This is not a reflection of reality but a reflection of our biases.

Past experiences, too, can shape our intuition.

Our intuition might caution us against taking a similar risk if we've been burnt before. However, this doesn't mean that the risk is inherently bad—it simply means that we've had a negative experience in the past. In this case, our intuition is acting more like a protective barrier than a reliable guide.

Emotional scars can also influence our intuition. If we've been hurt, our intuition might urge us to avoid similar situations in the future. But this can prevent us from growing and learning. It's important to recognize when our intuition is being influenced by emotional scars and to take steps to heal these wounds.

Intuition: A Natural and Scientific Phenomenon

Often shrouded in an aura of mysticism, intuition is frequently misunderstood as a magical or supernatural phenomenon. However, the reality is far from this perception. Intuition, in its essence, is a natural and scientific process deeply rooted in the intricate workings of our brain.

Contrary to popular belief, intuition does not involve any supernatural forces or mystical powers. It is not a product of divine intervention or psychic abilities. Instead, it is a testament to our brain's remarkable capacity to process information at an astounding speed, far surpassing the pace of our conscious awareness.

Our brains constantly absorb and analyze information, even when we are not consciously aware of it. This continuous influx of information is processed at lightning speed, resulting in what we perceive as intuition. It is our brain's way of drawing on past experiences and knowledge to make quick, often accurate judgments about the present or future.

So, the next time you experience a 'gut feeling' or an 'instinctive' reaction, remember that it's not magic or supernatural. It's your brain doing what it does best – processing information and making connections at a speed that leaves our conscious mind in awe. Embrace your intuition, for it is a powerful tool honed by nature and science.

Recognizing Intuition

Understanding Intuition: A New Perspective

In the realm of human experiences, intuition often remains an enigma. It's a feeling, a hunch, a gut instinct that guides our decisions, often without us even realizing it. But what does intuition really feel like? How can we distinguish it from other internal experiences such as fear, desire, or rationalization? Understanding these nuances can provide us with a new perspective on this fascinating aspect of human cognition.

Intuitive insights are typically characterized by a sense of clarity. They are not clouded by emotional intensity or personal biases. Instead, they present themselves as clear, objective insights that seem to emerge from nowhere. This is one of the key factors that sets intuition apart from other internal experiences.

Desire and fear, for instance, are often accompanied by strong emotional responses. Whether it's the excitement of a new opportunity or the anxiety of a potential threat, these experiences are usually marked by a heightened emotional state. Intuition, on the other hand, is more subtle. It comes with a sense of certainty and urgency but without the emotional intensity.

Moreover, rationalization involves a conscious process of reasoning and justification. We weigh the pros and cons, analyze the potential outcomes, and make a decision based on logical reasoning. Intuition, however, bypasses this analytical process. It provides us with immediate insights without the need for conscious deliberation.

How can we cultivate this intuitive insight?

The first step is awareness. By understanding intuition's distinct characteristics, we can become more attuned to its presence in our daily lives. We can learn to recognize the clear, neutral insights that emerge from our subconscious mind and use them to guide our decisions and actions.

Understanding intuition is not just about recognizing its presence. It's about harnessing its power. By learning to trust our intuitive insights, we can make more informed decisions, navigate complex situations easily, and ultimately lead a more fulfilling life.

When to Trust Your Intuition

Trusting Your Intuition: A Balanced Approach

In the hustle and bustle of our fast-paced world, we often find ourselves grappling with decisions that require quick thinking and swift action. Amidst this whirlwind of decision-making, one tool that often gets overlooked is our intuition. Trusting your intuition means tuning into that inner voice that whispers wisdom and guidance. However, it's not as simple as blindly following that voice. It's about striking a balance between intuition and rational thought, especially when the stakes are high.

Intuition is a powerful tool that can guide us in unexpected ways. That gut feeling nudges you towards or away from a certain path. It's the inexplicable sense of knowing something without concrete evidence. However, while intuition can be a valuable guide, it should not be the sole basis for our decisions. Instead, it should serve as a prompt for further inquiry and investigation.

It's crucial to balance intuition with rational thought in complex situations involving significant consequences. This doesn't mean dismissing your intuition; rather, it means acknowledging it and applying logical analysis to the situation. Doing so allows you to consider all aspects of the situation, leading to a more informed and balanced decision.

So, how do we strike this balance? It starts with listening to your intuition and respecting its wisdom. Then, take a step back and assess the situation rationally. Ask questions, gather facts, and weigh the pros and cons. Intuition and rational thought are not mutually exclusive; they can and should work together to guide you toward the best possible outcome.

Trusting your intuition doesn't mean ignoring logic and reason. It means using all the tools at your disposal - your intuition, your rational mind, and your ability to gather and analyze information - to make the best possible decisions. So, the next time you're faced with a tough decision, remember to trust your intuition, but don't forget to balance it with rational thought.

Integrating Intuition

Integrating Intuition and Rational Analysis for Effective Decision-Making

In the bustling business world, decision-making often feels like a high-stakes chess game. Every move counts, and one wrong turn can lead to a cascade of unfortunate events. In such a scenario, how does one make the right call? The answer lies in a balanced approach that integrates intuition with rational analysis.

Intuition, often dismissed as a whimsical whisper of the mind, has a crucial role in decision-making. It ignites the flame of insight, the gut feeling that nudges us toward a particular direction when we stand at a decision-making crossroads. However, to make the most of this intuitive wisdom, it needs to be integrated with rational analysis.

Rational thought serves as the test for the hypotheses generated by intuition. It weighs the alternatives, considers potential consequences, and meticulously tests the insights provided by intuition. This integration of intuition and rational thought leads to a more holistic approach to decision-making, one that considers both a situation's emotional and logical aspects.

This balanced approach can lead to more effective decision-making. It allows for a wider range of perspectives and a deeper understanding of the situation at hand. By harnessing the power of both intuition and rational thought, decision-makers can navigate the complex landscape of business with greater confidence and precision.

The key to effective decision-making lies in integrating intuition and rational analysis. It is not a matter of choosing one over the other but rather of using each to its full potential in a harmonious dance of decision-making. So, the next time you find yourself at a crossroads, remember to listen to your intuition and test its wisdom with rational thought.

Intuition: A Powerful Lens to View the World

Intuition is a unique and powerful lens through which we view the world. Far from being a supernatural phenomenon, intuition is a natural cognitive ability that everyone possesses.

Understanding and respecting intuition's role in our lives can help us use it wisely and effectively. This cognitive ability, often underestimated, is a tool that can guide us through life, helping us make decisions and understand situations beyond the reach of our conscious minds.

Intuition is not about predicting the future or having a sixth sense. It's about understanding the world around us on a deeper level. It's about recognizing patterns and making connections that our conscious mind might miss. It's about trusting our gut feelings and following our instincts.

Acknowledging and harnessing our intuitive abilities can enhance our decision-making skills, improve our relationships, and navigate life with greater confidence and clarity. Intuition is not a replacement for rational thought but a complement to it. It provides a different perspective and a different way of knowing and understanding the world.

So, let's respect and appreciate our intuition, not as a mystical force but as a natural and powerful cognitive ability. Let's learn to trust our gut feelings and follow our instincts. Let's use our intuition wisely and effectively as a powerful lens through which to view the world.

JULIE FAIRHURST

"A woman knows by intuition or instinct
what is best for herself."
Marilyn Monroe

2

EMILY

"Existence speaks to us through synchronicities, the mysterious coincidences that are always showing us the next steps to take on our evolutionary journeys."
Rumi

In life, you experience little synchronicities and internal intuition. Our job as sentient beings is to pick up on these little gifts or blessings from the universe. Sometimes, you meet another person, and your intuition says, "This person is important," whether it be as a best friend, lover, or a lesson for growth.

At some capacity, you were meant to meet; your paths both brought you to this moment in time. At the most profound level of consciousness, our mind says, "There you are, I've been waiting."

As sentient beings, we can experience positive and negative feelings like pleasure, joy, pain, and distress. These experiences shape a person's development and are directly created by either ignoring or following your intuition. Learning to be more in tune with picking up on these frequencies is pivotal to finding true happiness.

Taking the time to ask Is this interaction making me feel good? Respected? Or am I ignoring my gut to satisfy my needs? Listening to your heart and mind. Trust your gut and dive wholeheartedly into every interaction while remembering that everything is an experience; nothing belongs to you.

Maintain the boundary that other people have an intuition of their own to respect. "free will." Everyone is living a life as complex as our own. We may never know how much of an influence the things we say or do affect others, but we can choose how we respond internally to that gut feeling.

Am I staying true to myself and allowing others to be true to their own intuitions? Are we helping each other grow? Are we walking each other home?

Below, I'm sharing a poem I wrote about meeting someone and immediately feeling a spark.

Bonfire. Bonfire You,
Burns so bright,
Fire so big,
Light up my night,
Let your Flames caress,
Singe my curves,
Smoke takes my breath,
Lose my words.
Kindling kisses,
Fiery heat,
Eyes like,
Amber on cedar,
Nectar so sweet.
Burnt finger tips,
The scent in my hair,
Cold spring night,
Love in the air.

"God gave women intuition and femininity. Used properly, the combination easily jumbles the brain of any man I've ever met."
Farrah Fawcett

3

SABRINA LAMBERT

"Trusting your intuition means tuning in as deeply as you can to the energy you feel, following that energy moment to moment, trusting that it will lead you where you want to go and bring you everything you desire."
Shakti Gawain

Learning to Trust My Inner Woo

Of course, as a young girl with a newly minted driver's license, I could not explain why I was able to narrowly miss hitting a car halfway in the ditch and halfway in my lane on an icy back-country road.

As the danger approached, my first instinct as an inexperienced driver was to stomp on the brake, yet a quieter feeling had me release the accelerator and gently turn the steering wheel away from the ditched car. I remember holding my breath while the sound of slow-motion air swished between the cars' fenders. I was safe.

Some would say it was the lessons I learned while attending a professional driving school to prepare for passing the driving test, but it was more than that, as it happened without me thinking.

The next time I smacked into my inner guide was a normal morning when I went to get my three-year-old daughter out of bed and ready to go to daycare. She had a low fever and was fussy and whimpering about her tummy hurting. Usually, she wanted Mommy hugs when she did not feel well, but the moment I attempted to embrace her, she cried out, "No, Mommy! Don't Touch. I hurt!"

I started to list in my head what she might have eaten the day before that could bother her stomach so much. I asked my husband if he thought it was a flu, yet the feeling in my gut said this was more serious. Being three, what could it be?

My little girl was not her usual energetic, happy self. I called our doctor, who was a 45-minute car ride away, and she said to come in for a check. The check-up expanded to see a pediatrician in the same building. That visit resulted in rushing our girl to Children's Hospital emergency with suspected Appendicitis. I am glad I did not wait to see the doctor.

My Inner Woo has also been there whenever I have needed support with my own health or that of my husband. Even though we both have navigated some serious health issues, needing hospitalization and surgery, that calm, quiet knowing was there, reinforcing that the situation was temporary and that all would be ok.

I do believe that my Inner Woo was a passenger with me as I was stopped in busy traffic behind a vehicle waiting to turn left. I glanced in the rearview mirror and was horrified to watch the grill of a one ton truck racing towards me. Intellectually, I knew I had nowhere to go that would not put me further in harm's way. I could feel panic filling my body, tensing my muscles, anticipating the impact, when a voice whispered, "Don't brace. Take a deep breath; relax on impact."

Amazingly, what felt like ages was only seconds. The truck rear-ended my car, which then bounced against the vehicle in front of me. My car and I were the icing in the cookie sandwich.

Even though my car was bent beyond repair, I, along with the other driver, was shaken but uninjured. No whiplash and no sore or bruised muscles were evident even a few days later. I was saved by my trust in my Inner Woo.

Now, in the second half of my life, my Woo seems more prevalent than before. Maybe it is no longer drowned out by the busy noise of working and raising a family. Having more quiet time has amplified what I sense is the essence of who I really am and what I really want without the interference of the opinion of others, no matter how well-meaning.

Once I retired, my husband and I wanted to get out of the city and move into a smaller community without the three-hour rush of traffic, morning and night. We researched many apartments in three communities and finally whittled it down to two that were within four blocks of each other.

One was newer, in a large complex, and the other was larger, but a bit less modern, in a small four-plex, and cost a few dollars more monthly. Both would serve our needs, but which to choose? Even though it was slightly more rent, the one in the smaller building made me feel better about moving there. It felt safer, quieter. I also had a sense that it was a better opportunity to meet our neighbors.

My Woo was right. Eight months after we moved into our smaller complex, the larger building a few blocks away suffered a massive fire that was directly above the apartment we had been looking at. During the repairs, those unfortunate residents were out of their homes for over eighteen months.

I am grateful that we listened to our feelings. I am beginning to learn to cultivate my Inner Woo. I play with it, doing trivia quizzes. More often than not, my first feeling about the right answer, especially when I don't intellectually know it, is often the correct answer.

However, I am stubborn and still do not always listen to that feeling, which results in getting the answer incorrect. However, when the nudge comes about people in my life or decisions we want to make, I have learned to favor my Inner Woo.

My husband and I have recently picked up our household and moved back to my hometown, near the area where he grew up, to be closer to our immediate family members. Of course, the area no longer resembles that of our youth, but after a couple of years of vacationing there again, that quiet knowing told us, " 32 years away is enough. It's time to come back home." Certainly, a big household move is a painful sorting of what to keep, what to donate, and what to trash. And then there is the disrupted reorganization of our new living environment, getting what we kept to fit into the new rooms, closets, and cupboards, obtaining and putting together new unfamiliar furnishings that replaced what was old and discarded, and creating new routines for our life.

My loyal companion Woo is here too, calmly loving our choice. All is well and good.

"When I stopped to take a breath, I noticed I had wings."
Jodi Livon

4

NANCY BEAULIEU

"Energy flows where attention goes."
Michael Beckwith

How to raise your vibration. Why would someone want to raise their vibration? What does that even mean? How do we do that?

Each person in the world holds a vibration. It's like a frequency that we emit, kind of like a radio wave. With music, you can tune into country, metal, rock, rap, the blues, pop, dance, etc. Each radio station might make you feel a certain way. You might even describe the blues, rap, or metal as low frequency and dance as high frequency. Your mood and attitude have everything to do with your vibration. If you ever notice that you're having a bad day, you might also notice that you seem to be attracting more bad throughout your day.

You can change the channel, so to speak. If you react in a big way to the "bad" things happening to you, you will stay on the same channel. If you notice the first bad thing that happened to you, notice your feelings, and then become an observer of the situation and reflect on any lessons, then you are one step closer to a better day.

It's perfectly fine to feel your feelings, but don't let them take over you. Taking yourself out of the victim mindset and into the student mindset is one quick way to raise your vibration. Another quick way to rise up even higher is to name ten things you're grateful for. You can phrase it like this: Thank you for clean drinking water, thank you, thank you, thank you. When you say thank you three times in a row, that seems to be the magic number. You amplify your vibration even more when you write your gratitude down.

You feel more joy, peace, and love when your vibration is higher. Operating at a higher frequency helps you manifest a more positive experience. When we fill our own "cup" up high, we can overflow to a point where we can then be of service to others.

Practicing self-care is another way to raise your vibration. With self-care, you want to keep on top of what's good for your mind, body, and soul. Your mind might enjoy reading, doing crosswords, playing a game, listening to a podcast, or some other type of learning. Your body is going to benefit from adequate water intake, proper nutrition, exercise, stretching, movement, sunlight, fresh air, and possibly skin-care and haircare.

Your soul may benefit from singing, listening to music, dancing, laughing, connecting with a friend, giving hugs, viewing beauty, meditation, or doing any form of art. You'll know what your soul desires.

If you're in your home, you can raise your vibration by diffusing essential oils, burning incense, lighting a nice, scented candle, or creating a wonderful environment with aromas. Sometimes, opening up all the windows and sageing or simply just refreshing the air in your home is what's needed. You will likely find that by tidying up your space, you will feel better as well.

Certain colors might make you feel a certain way as well. Be mindful of what decor you have up or what colors you wear. Crystals in your space or on you (jewelry) will also elevate you. Sound will affect you as well, so turn on some positive music to lift you up.

I typically find higher frequency music to play on YouTube with channels such as @awakenation @inner-healing @innerlotusmusic @meditativemind @musicforbodyandspirit and play it loud enough to put sound vibrations throughout my home.

The energy in your home can become stale without fresh air or sound. Even simply clapping breaks up energy and changes its state.

What are you wearing? Are your clothes uncomfortable or restrictive, or do they make you feel like a slob? Put on something that makes you feel beautiful or comfortable.

Have you had enough rest lately? Most people need at least seven hours of sleep. Sleep improves mood, which in turn greatly improves vibration.

Have you ever been mindful of your breathing? Take a deep breath through your nose and blow it out your mouth. Do this three times. You're reconnecting with your body and calming yourself down. You can also do chakra-balancing meditations to keep your spiritual body in alignment. Yoga is also great for that. Simply hanging upside down or touching your toes resets your nervous system.

When was the last time you played? Have you done anything a child would do lately? Your inner child will thank you. Have you ever hugged a tree and thanked it? When did you last visit a waterfall or a body of water? When was the last time you hugged another human? Did you know a hug is supposed to last more than 20 seconds?

Have you set any goals lately and worked towards them? Have you ever done any healing work? Everyone's childhood has some trauma that maybe hasn't been dealt with. Have you forgiven yourself for anything you did in the past or forgiven other people who have wronged you? Apologies with zero expectations can help you feel better.

Do you know what Reiki, Access Bars, or acupuncture are? Why not try something new? Do you speak kind words to yourself? Positive affirmations go a long way. Are you in need of a shower?

A shower is a super fast way to raise your energy. Do you have clutter around your home that you could donate or sell? Have you ever volunteered before? Do you read the news, listen to true crime podcasts, or watch horror?

If you do, maybe replace it with something that makes you laugh or feel inspired. Who do you hang out with? Do they make you feel good? Are you seen, heard, supported, and valued? Changing your friends might be in order as well. It's pretty easy to tell if something makes you feel better or worse. Better is high vibrational, and worse is low vibrational. We don't need to be in a place of judgment of others or ourselves, but we can strive to do better.

Self-improvements are all ways to change our energy. Choosing too many steps at once might overwhelm you, so start with one or two things listed above to raise your vibe. As you raise it and become comfortable, challenge yourself to add more changes. Keep going at a pace that you can live with.

Eventually, you will fall in love with yourself and your life, and you'll be amazed at just how easy it is to become a better version of yourself. You will manifest more intensely and more positively.

Who knows, maybe you'll raise your vibration so high you can speak to the spirit world and sense the communication coming back. That is where I'm at with my energy. I do have dips in energy, so I remain mindful and focused on raising it. The study of energy is something we Mediums do, and I've just shared many tips with you.

I hope this hugely helps you. With love from Fancy Nancy!

"Faith requires following the power of a whisper."
Shannon L. Alder

5

BRENDA COOPER

"Intuition is the compass of the soul."
Anonymous

INTUITION WHISPERS

In whispers soft, intuition speaks,
A silent guide, when reason's weak,
Beyond the senses, it ushers you through,
An inner compass will guide you true.

In quiet moments, it softly calls,
A hidden strength when uncertainty stalls,
It knows the truths that words can't tel,l
In its whispers, your secrets dwell.

No need for proof or logic's mind,
Intuition flickers its light-defined,
In shadows deep in the dim-lit light,
It steers us true through the darkest night.

Through intuition's silent grace,
We find solace in its warm embrace,
A hidden language of the heart's domain,
Revealing truths words cannot explain.

Trust the stirring, that inner song,
For intuition knows where you belong,
To futures unseen, where dreams come true,
Intuition will always see you through.

So heed the whispers, the intuition's call,
It knows the way, it won't let you fall,
In the chambers of your heart, it resides,
A faithful compass that's your true guide.

"I throw a spear into the darkness. That is intuition.
Then, I must send an army into the darkness to find the spear.
That is intellect."
Ingmar Bergman

6

SHERON CHISHOLM

"I am smart and wise, for I have a genius inside of me. I trust my wisdom, and I enjoy learning." Doreen Virtue

Today, I went to my gynecologist to get the results of my surgical procedure. I was by myself, and I remember his voice was very caring, and his face was very serious.

As he talked, I felt like I had turned my feelings off. I responded stoically and agreed to further surgery. It was a little more serious this time, but I still remember feeling very calm and not registering what was about to happen.

The cancer was quite pervasive in terms of the organs involved and would require removal of all organs, total hysterectomy, and involve an incision rather than a scope since they did not know if there was any migration of the cancer to the peritoneum.

I felt scared at this point, and of course, my mind went to thoughts of, "Do I have long to live?"

After I left the doctor's office, I went to my car and started to cry while talking to God." What am I going to do now, God?" I just adopted Kayla, "What was going to happen to her?' What was she going to think?" I worried about what would happen to her and what she would think.

My daughter was only with me for nine months. She looked at me with fear, asking, "What's going to happen to me?" She meant what was going to happen when I was in the hospital and also what if I didn't live long enough for her to be on her own. I could answer part of her question, but not all. Of course, I had to wait until after surgery to answer the rest of her questions.

After we talked, she said she was good with the answer but still had the fear of being alone again and having to go back to foster care. That was a concern for both of us. I felt guilty for being sick and putting her in this situation. There wasn't much I could tell her, but I did say that God had allowed me to adopt her, and He was going to be with me and her through this.

The other question on my mind was that I had planned a trip with my daughter and Goddaughter for a graduation gift that I had promised my Goddaughter a year or so before. It was all paid for it, and arrangements were made.

I was unsure what would happen since it was early in this event. It was a wait-and-see situation.

I discussed this with Erica's parents, who were very good friends, and their immediate response was," We will come up and be with you and take care of Kayla so she isn't so scared." I was relieved immediately. The trip was not their immediate concern, but I was. They were such good friends, and I felt very loved.

There was one more obstacle, and that was telling my father. He was with his new wife in the area, so I thought he would stay for my surgery. He said that he would not be staying. He had to take his wife to visit her daughter in South Carolina.

I let him know it was okay and that he needed to do what he thought was right.

I knew it would be difficult since my mom had died of cancer some three years before. He did decide to stay until I was home from the hospital. I had many feelings about this because I felt he should have responded with an immediate expression of sadness and concern for me, but he did not. That made me feel lonely, angry, and afraid of facing this all by myself.

"The more you trust your intuition, the more empowered you become, the stronger you become, and the happier you become."
Gisele Bundchen

7

RHONDA FUNK

"The true test of character is not how much we know how to do, but
how we behave when we don't know what to do."
John Holt

A Walk In The Park Hey, where did you go?

On a Journey with my thoughts,
A mind wandering on its own;
Navigating a dark, familiar street with a swaying light post;
An empty park bench and a threat of rain,
Vehicles are like my thoughts.

Zoom past, leaving only the quick memories of
light streaks behind.
Chilled. Lonely but oddly content, I walk.
Where did I go, you ask?
On an adventure made for emotions.

Where gravity is like concrete to my soul.
Anchoring my heart as the wind blows;
Uplifting the flower pedals,
And fallen leaves.

Into a spiral suspended in time.
Where Chaos... and Peace dance the tango!
For what was well known is challenged by the whisper of a breeze.
So... Where have I truly been?

Here. Holding this hot cup of tea,
That calmly stings my palms,
In an attempt to bring warmth to the chill within,
Processing, Anxiously anticipating answers, I intensely feel,
As I stand here looking out the window, listening,
for myself as I return from my walk in the park.

"Intuition will tell the thinking mind where to look next."
Jonas Salk

8

ANNA AU

"Instead of worrying about what you cannot control, shift your
energy to what you can create."
Roy T. Bennett

My Three Wishes

Should we stay or should we go? Should we stay for familiarities or
leave for possibilities? The decision I made has changed our lives.

When my older son ("H") was diagnosed with autism on New Year's
2000, the millennial celebration was the last thing that was on my
mind. Struggling with all the behavioral issues and taking care of my
newborn son, I was exhausted with anger, fear, fatigue, shame, and,
most of all, helplessness.

My B.A. in Psychology sure didn't prepare me for the term "Autism."
Fortunately, there was new research in autism and Behavioral
Consultants available in California, USA.

Wow, I considered hitting a jackpot. At that time, there were no
autism-related services available in British Columbia. As high as the

US exchange rate was, I chose to hire the US Consultant and had a program in place.

In February 2000, a team of four aides were hired and started working with H 40 hours per week. With limited funding from the province, I had to cash in all my savings and more.... After two years of therapy, there were improvements in H. Then, I was not ready to face another surprise. My second son ("A") was also diagnosed with autism.

Suddenly, I was running two teams of aides, 40 hours per week. In my mind, what was the alternative? So, full steam ahead with this new arrangement for two more years. Honestly, I cannot remember much about how we survived those four years of having aides in and out of my house. I was still working full-time; fortunately, my parents were helping with the boys during the day and on weekends.

Oh, I almost forgot to mention about my marriage. It was a disaster ever since the first diagnosis and ended with disappointments. To top it off, our financial situation was worsening, and bankruptcy was the only way to get us out of the financial hole we were in. Given the limited funding available from the province, there was no way we could keep funding the programs privately.

H was eight, and A was four at the time. The school system didn't have any professionally trained staff to oversee autistic children. To be inclusive in a regular class had become exclusive outside the class-room, with an aide trying to keep the "peace" for the other students. Most of the school days for H were cut short because of the school's limited resources. Fortunately, A was only four and was not in grade school yet. Then, I started to realize there would not be any future for them at school. A little voice in my head started to blink: There must be something better somewhere other than B.C.

Alberta! They had the best provincial funding and specialized programs for autistic children. We only needed to move one province over. Not that simple. Jobs and housing, and both my husband and I worked full-time. Still, I thought he could get a teaching job in Alberta, and we could sell our house and buy one there. I could find a job. Why wouldn't it work? The response from him was: "I don't want to move. I have always been a B.C. boy." So be it! I decided to do it all by myself.

There were three wishes, and if only all of them came true.

- First wish: Keep my current job, which I just started a year ago.
- Second wish: I want to get my share of equity from the sale of the house so I can buy a house in Alberta.
- Third wish: Get a mortgage and a car loan.

I could then move to Alberta and start a new life with my boys. All three wishes came true in 2004, and so in May 2005, I moved to Edmonton with my boys.

For the last 19 years, they graduated from high school, attended programs and college, met new friends, obtained a driver's license, worked part-time, and lived their lives fully as much as they like to. The skies are the limit.

Raising them by myself in a different province has not been an easy journey. I sometimes wondered what would have happened if we hadn't moved. I didn't let fear take over my determination to get the best treatment and learning for the boys.

Some of my friends, including my own family, thought I was crazy for doing it alone. It's so worth it watching them become nice, fine young men. That's more than anything I would have wanted. I have absolutely no regrets. It's not about me anymore when it comes to my children.

That little voice was the best thing that happened to me, and the decision to follow that voice has worked out perfectly for us.

My belief is: Do the right thing, and everything will turn out the way it should be!

"Follow your intuition, listening to your dreams,
your inner voice to guide you."
Kartori Hall

9

ANGELA RUNQUIST

"The intuitive mind is a sacred gift, and the rational mind is a faithful servant. We have created a society that honors the servant and has forgotten the gift."
Albert Einstein

Proverbs 3:5-6 NKJV - Trust in the Lord with all your heart, and lean not on your own understanding; In all your ways acknowledge Him, and He shall direct your paths.

I am a proud mom of three amazing kids and Nana to six awesome grandchildren.

When my children were young, my world drastically changed. My marriage fell apart, and instead of being a stay-at-home mom and Pastor's wife, I quickly became a single parent and the sole provider.

There were many times over the years when I needed to trust my God-given intuition. Several of those times included relocating my family and starting over.

I was recently talking with one of my daughters and she reminded me about one those intuitive decisions that led to a very positive experience for all of us. I had needed to relocate my family in order to continue to provide for them. The job I was working in Dresden TN, wasn't paying enough to provide for our needs. My savings was quickly running out from trying to keep up.

I saw my only choices were moving into a low-income apartment full of drug use or moving back to Iowa with my parents. I prayed for direction. I took my family on a weekend trip to visit a pastor friend and his church family. Before I shared our financial situation with him, he asked me what it would take to get me to move there.

We are a low-maintenance family, so I told him all I needed was a job and a home for my family.

He quickly became an answer to prayer when he said he could provide both the job and the home. This move took us to Fayetteville, TN, where I taught in the private school in the church, and our home was located right there behind the church building. This position came with paid tuition for my children, a home, and year-round pay.

Since I had some time off in the summer, I felt led to do something special as a family. After talking to a missionary couple and my pastor, I decided that my kids and I would go on a family mission trip. I sent out letters to churches, family, and friends to introduce our plans and ask for prayer and financial support. The Lord provided for every aspect of this ministry adventure.

Before becoming a single parent, I was very dependent on my husband: I didn't drive far from home, and I didn't make many decisions on my own. I had to quickly grow up and learn to do things on my own. I had to learn to trust God with our needs. I also had to learn that it's ok to ask for help from others.

We began to plan our trip. Our mission trip focus was at a little church on the Ute Mountain Ute Reservation in Towaoc, CO. We were going to help our missionary friends with their Vacation Bible School program for the Ute children. This was such a big step for me that I would never have thought about making a trip of this magnitude. Driving a nearly 24-hour trip each way was totally out of my comfort zone. But God... He gave me peace about all of it.

We made plans to be gone for a month. I loaded up my cooler so we could picnic along the way to save money on food. Packed up my van with four kids, ages 7 to 12, and all their things. Yes, I said four kids. My oldest daughter brought along a friend for our journey. We started out fully protected by prayer.

We stopped at a hotel along the way to sleep, but the lady took one look at me and the kids and said I couldn't afford to stay there and refused to provide us with a room even though I was prepared to pay. We found a rest area and slept in the van. We made the best out of a rough situation, and the kids went on an adventure. We safely made it to Towaoc, CO, and stayed in our friend's camper for the next few weeks.

My two oldest joined me and the missionary couple in working to make the Vacation Bible School a success, while the two younger ones enjoyed being a part of everything with the Ute children. I helped with the lessons, skits, crafts, and snacks, and the older girls helped with snacks, crafts, and games. One of my favorite moments with my kids that week was playing with the Native American children and having a frosting fight while preparing one of the snacks. I enjoyed every moment of that week and looked forward to the rest of our adventures.

During the week we were there, I was concerned about something being wrong with my van, so I had it checked out. Once again, the Lord provided and protected us from what could have been a disaster later on while traveling home. I had made plans to visit a few friends while out in the Four Corners area.

I took the kids to Blanding, Utah, where we had lived for five years and previously served on the mission field. We saw the Four Corners Monument, a Navajo Tribal Park where four states meet: Arizona, New Mexico, Colorado, and Utah. We then took a few days to drive to Moab, Utah, to visit a church and friends there and the unique "Hole N," the Rock home found along the roadside between Blanding and Moab.

We made it back to TN and were excited to share with our church family and friends all about our adventures and our time serving on the Ute Reservation. Nearly 20 years later, my children, now all grown and married with their own families, still talk about that trip. I am so glad I didn't let fear rule my heart. Instead, I trusted the Lord and followed His leading. Trust in Him with all your heart, your life, and your family.

"Being able to put your blinders on, ignore negative opinions, and follow your strong intuition is what's validating to me. It's a great feeling to know you can trust your gut."
Whitney Wolfe Herd

10

LETICIA RODRIGUEZ

"Intuition is the bridge between the soul and the ego's thoughts and sensations. If one can remain unidentified with thoughts and sensations, and without being unconscious, he will know through the development of intuition the nature of the soul."
Paramahansa Yogananda

I've always been highly intuitive. In fact, my knack for picking up on "bad vibes" has been known to raise goosebumps on the arms of those who've witnessed it. It's not something I do intentionally. I'm just sensitive to certain frequencies. But I didn't always recognize this at the moment as my intuition spoke to me.

In the past, I'd receive intuitive hits, but I'd either misinterpret them or my ego would create excuses to deny them. It was the latter critical error that led me into an abusive relationship with a manipulative partner – I distinctly felt the warning signals in my heart and stomach, but my mind convinced me to dismiss them. The funny thing is the universe will deliver whatever is necessary to wake you up. Now, I no longer ignore it when my internal *danger!* alarm goes off, although I am still learning to trust when the nudges are guiding me toward something beneficial.

Intuition can present itself in different ways for each of us. There are several "clairsenses" that every one of us can tap into; it's simply a matter of being open to aligning with these abilities.

Some people are better at knowing (Claircognizance), while some are better at feeling (clairsentience). Some can hear messages (clairaudience) or visualize them (clairvoyance).

It's important to understand that these occurrences are not an indication of mental instability or delusion.

All humans possess these innate abilities. Men have them, too, although women tend to be more attuned to them, likely because we identify strongly with our feminine energy.

Try to think of a time when you had a "gut feeling" that proved to be true, averting you from a crisis. Or maybe you saw something seemingly coincidental – perhaps a billboard, animal, or vision in a dream – but, ironically, it was directly related to something you were processing at the time.

Or your attention was drawn to a lyric in a song that confirmed a decision you were debating. Sometimes intuitive messages arrive as subtle inspirations, sometimes they are blaringly obvious. Other times, they may seem irrelevant at first but end up leading you through a series of events that pave a path to a desired destination.

So, how do you "tap" into your intuition? I think there are two crucial truths to accept:

1. Your thoughts are not necessarily reality.
2. Everything is energy, including you.

The average human has around 60,000 thoughts per day, the majority being repetitions of thoughts from yesterday and thoughts of the future, which may or may not come to fruition. Some thoughts are serene or helpful, while others are turbulent, mere noise. Thoughts arise from our ego's conditioning (everything we've been taught by our parents, teachers, government, friends, social media, etc.) and our past traumas.

The 3D world around us, coupled with the schemas we've developed, trigger our egos constantly. Triggers stimulate the ego to create thoughts, which then induce emotions. The deeper the emotion is felt, the more those schemas become ingrained within us because the ego thrives on identifying with them. However, the essence of who we truly are lies beyond the transient mental formations of our egos. The key is to understand and embrace the notion that the narrative our ego creates is not our core identity.

Intuition is the whisper beneath the ego's chatter, the silent awareness of an energetic presence within our physical body. When you listen to it, it guides you in the direction of your highest good. I think the biggest challenge is to detach from what the ego wants us to think and feel and instead acknowledge and explore our natural inclinations, our gut instincts. This may require considerable practice to master; we must first catch the automatic thoughts that arise, observe the emotion that follows, detach from the emotion, and feel the energy within to decipher the message coming through.

Some grounding practices that have helped me familiarize myself with my own internal guidance system include journaling, yoga, therapy, time spent outside in nature, connecting with animals, taking periodic mental vacations from social media, reading books on self-help and spirituality, spending more time with uplifting people and less with those who affect my energy unfavorably.

I've also found that certain spiritual practices have helped me tune into my subconscious on a deeper level and have allowed me to control my anxious responses to stressors better. Some of my favorite spiritual practices include sound baths, reiki, meditation, working with crystals and tarot, and connecting with like-minded people at various stages in their spiritual journeys.

Exploring and thoroughly analyzing my past - my upbringing, my traumas, and even my successes -has given me great insight into what has influenced the development of my egoic self, my automatic responses, and how I show up for myself in my life. I am progressively healing my anxious attachment and co-dependent inner-child wounds. Doing this shadow work has been so important for finding peace in the present moment and learning how to re-direct my focus to creating more fulfillment in my life.

Intuition allows us to read the unspoken and grasp the unknowable— our "sixth sense." Infusing our actions with this underlying awareness guides us to live authentically, aligning us with our core values and desires and prompting us to make conscious choices harmoniously with our subconscious.

I hope we all learn to trust that inner voice and create our best days doing what makes us happy. The next time you feel pulled towards something that feels good, lean into it; this is your intuition saying, "Hell, YES!". The next time your alarm bells go off, take heed of that warning; your intuition is trying to guide you in another direction.

"Intuition is a sense of knowing how to act spontaneously,
without needing to know why."
Sylvia Clare

11

LINDA S NELSON

"Your inner voice is the voice of divinity. To hear it, we need to be in solitude, even in crowded places."
A.R. Rahman

Intuition—that still small voice. Can you hear it? Do you know how powerful your inner voice is? I didn't—or maybe I couldn't.

My life was so busy running a household, raising a family, and working in a stressful corporate job with LOTS of responsibility for a human resources department. I often had no time for ANYTHING but – survival! Looking back, I often think this must be on Satan's job description. Keep them so busy and distracted with the noise of everyday living that they can't hear God's still, small voice in all the noise.

I've discovered our intuition IS the voice of God. It is the place within us – our soul – where God can speak to us – if we're quiet. It's covered up and hard to hear in all the distractions we fall prey to while living our busy, unprioritized lives.

It's in the solitude – the quiet – the coming away with Him in those precious moments where we can hear Him. He uses His still, small voice to reach into the very depths of our being where He can speak to us.

I know that sounds very deep! Let me step back from it a bit.

Ever had those moments in the shower where there is no noise, no questions, no expectations of dealing with someone else's needs – if only for a few precious minutes? That may be where, in a moment, you get clarity, a fabulous idea, or an answer to a question you've been pondering. THAT is your inner voice trying to get your attention! It's there – waiting to be tapped into. IF you're just quiet!

And there's so much power there when you learn to trust it – and to trust God in that sacred place. There is a way to begin to trust that inner voice. And it took a forced pause moment in my life to discover it.

My mom had passed away after an intense, short battle with cancer. She was only 77 and was my best friend, mentor, and confidante. Even more importantly – she was my spiritual guide, and so her loss in my life left a huge void. I felt adrift in my world, which was crazy busy so much that I had difficulty returning to it.

In this time of processing grief, I made a conscious decision to FEEL the grief. I had been through a bout of depression for several years before my mom's death and was taking anti-depressants for it. Just a few weeks prior to her passing, I had gone through a long, difficult process of weaning off the drugs and knew it was going to be challenging to deal with my mother's death without them. Although it was difficult to take no drugs during this grieving process, I DID learn that there's a difference between depression (a condition) and sadness (a result of living). And that was an important lesson for me to learn.

This decision to stay off drugs and feel the grief seemed to come to me from deep within myself. I didn't know if I could trust it. I questioned – were these my thoughts? Or God's thoughts? Was I wise to follow it? Even though I was "forced" to spend time in silence, I am so glad I did. This forced pause in my life caused me to slow down – and intentionally pull back from a life that left little time to be in solitude.

During this grief process, I had a hard time dealing with crowds – with people in general. It's not a good thing for someone whose career in human resources was ALL about people. Other people! Not me. I felt a huge nudge just to BE – not DO. As a people pleaser and high achiever, this was extremely difficult. I had a history of taking care of everyone else except for me. Until circumstances – or forced pauses came into my life to make ME a priority.

I'm still learning – as it's so easy to slip back into the familiar – even if it's harmful. I've had several other reminders or "forced pauses" to reconsider my life when I find myself slipping into my old patterns of DOING instead of BEING. It seems I learn lessons the hard way.

The pause surrounding my mother's death came after a depression or mental episode. But I've had forced pauses with physical ramifications, too. I can be so "other" oriented that I totally neglect myself – until my body stops me like it did several years ago with a heart episode. And once again, I needed to pause, reflect, and re-evaluate my priorities. I once again needed to find that balance of doing and being – which comes from tapping into my intuition.

The good news is that I recognize it sooner now than I did before. And I intentionally create times of silence to reset. I spend conscious time being silent. Something I now crave. I started small. I carved out a few minutes in the morning just for me. I gradually increased my time to a half hour – and eventually an hour – just for me and my God.

I started journaling. I started by writing one to three things I was grateful for each and every day. I blocked out this time on the calendar as "ME TIME," and it started my day off empowered! I'm so glad I began to listen to that inner voice – my intuition – that was covered up for so long.

I learned to trust my inner voice – my intuition – the place where I found peace even if I didn't understand everything at that moment. And gradually, I learned to trust that the voice I was hearing was MY voice – along with God's.

You see, I began to understand that He wants what's best for me. He will guide my steps towards the best path for me to take – if I only listen. That still small voice inside me? I can hear it!

"Intuition is a spiritual faculty and does not explain,
but simply points the way."
Florence Scovel Shinn

12

JULIE FAIRHURST

"If you're reading this... Congratulations, you're alive.
If that's not something to smile about,
then I don't know what is."
Chad Sugg

This is my story of ignoring my gut feeling and allowing a situation to escalate into a frightening event in my life. Trusting one's intuition is crucial as it often serves as an inner warning system that can help prevent undesirable outcomes. Ignoring these instincts can lead to dire consequences.

I spent 34 years as a successful real estate agent. Achieving success in this field required me to promote myself actively. This involved strategically marketing my services through various channels within my budget.

Bus benches, bus shelters, newspapers, the internet, thousands of mail-outs, flyer drops, TV advertising, social media, and more. If you are in business for yourself, selling your service, you'll understand what needs to happen if you want to achieve the ultimate success that just a few achieve.

You can imagine that if you make an effort to have your face everywhere, you are going to attract all sorts of people, mostly nice, kind people who want to hire you to help them with their life-changing moves. But there are also the not-so-nice people.

My stalker situation started in the evening, after midnight when my cell phone rang. I answered it only to have silence on the other end and then heavy breathing. I immediately hung up; it was an unknown number.

I ignored it and went about my life until it happened about two weeks later. Late at night, that unknown number was calling again. It was the same thing: silence and then that heavy breathing. This time, I used some offensive language and told the person off before I hung up.

The calls would come from time to time, and the same process would happen. Now, you may wonder why I answered. I didn't have a home phone, and I had young adults and teenagers, so I kept my phone on and did not put it on silence.

After this had gone on for over a year, and I had just hung up and ignored it, I got a voice message on my phone. I didn't hear it ring.

The voice was a male with an English-sounding accent. He proceeded to tell me he was going to kidnap me, tie me up, pour honey on me, and so on....

I immediately called the non-emergency number for the local RCMP. I was put on hold for a very long time, which was frustrating. So, I decided to go to the local station and speak with an officer.

When I arrived at the station, I was directed to a phone and told to call the non-emergency number. I started dialing and thought, I'm not going through this again. I held my phone up in the air and raised my voice, "I'm not leaving until someone listens to this."

I was told to sit and wait until an officer was free. About an hour later, an off-duty female officer called me to speak with me.

I explained everything. She took notes. Then she listened to the message. The first words out of her mouth were, "Do you live alone?" I told her that I did, and it was a little rancher very accessible if someone really wanted to break in. She told me to find somewhere else to stay and not go home.

She then left me in the interview room and told me she'd have another officer come and speak to me.

After about half an hour, a male police officer came into the interview room and spoke with me. I again explained everything to him. This time, though, before listening to the voice message on my phone, he asked me personal questions.

After my "interrogation," he listened to the voice message, and I saw the notes he made as he listened. Heavy breathing, kidnap, masturbation, and so on. Once he finished listing, he apologized for asking me so many personal questions. He explained that there are women who "make up stories" to get their ex's in trouble.

As the calls continued coming from an unknown number, he needed to call my phone service provider to see if they would release the number to them. First, they said, "No, the police need a warrant to get the information released." The office then put me on the phone, and I had to tell my service provider I was afraid for my life. Only then did they give the officer the information he'd asked for.

I went home, and within a few hours, they got him. He actually lived within walking distance of my home! He was 24 years old and had moved from England, thus the English accent.

I was told he was charged with Criminal Harassment and cried like a baby when they put the handcuffs on him. I was then told that I was not his only victim; he was doing it to a female mortgage broker, as well. They could not charge him with her case as they couldn't prove it.

While all this was happening, I recalled a conversation with a male recently with an English accent who inquired about viewing a home I had for sale. This is what scared me the most! What if?

The end to all this was that he was convicted and spent some time in jail, but most importantly, he is and will always be on a sexual offender list for life.

What does all this have to do with women's intuition? I felt it. I was being nudged all the time after every call. Even friends told me to go to the police earlier. But I consider myself a strong woman, not afraid of much, and I was extremely busy, so I pushed it all off and ignored it.

Despite the warnings and signs, I chose NOT to trust my instincts and carried on with my daily routine. Little did I know that listening to that inner voice could have potentially prevented a dangerous situation. It's crucial to acknowledge and respect the power of intuition, especially when it comes to personal safety and well-being.

If you have that "gut feeling," listen to it. Don't dismiss it as nothing. It may save your life.

"That is what the intuition is for:
it is the direct messenger of the soul."
Clarissa Pinkola Estes

13

HEATHER SCOTT

"Everything is revealed beforehand,
but only to those with eyes to see."
Michael Bassey Johnson

*Intuitive*Intuition*Premonition*

Premonition is like a warning from the future, a sense of something about to happen, often a feeling of dread or anticipation.

Intuition on the other hand, is more like a gut feeling or inner knowing about what is right or true, often without conscious reasoning or logical explanation. You know when you get that gut feeling that someone is watching you, can be a bit unsettling.

I worked at an insurance office in a mall in Whalley, Surrey, British Columbia. On my break, I would go to a food fair and sit "quietly," lol, by myself.

There were a lot of recovering addicts in the area who hung out at the food fair. I came to realize that it was a man named Brian who was watching me. I found it in me to approach him, and I said, "I am not sure if you realize what you are doing; you are watching me, and it is making me uncomfortable." He looked dumbfounded.

I went back to work, and later, he came into the office, and when he was approached by a co-worker, he said, "No, I want to talk to her", pointing at me. I approached, and he thanked me for having the courage to approach him; in fact, he didn't realize what he was doing.

Brian was relentless. He came in on a regular basis asking me out, and I would say no, and off he would go. This went on for months before I gave in. We dated and eventually ended up living in the same apartment building and eventually moving in together, which was 24 years ago. As mentioned in an earlier Women Like Me book, "The Warrior Within," the relationship was amazing until it wasn't. I digress!

Background on Brian: he had spent 13 years on Vancouver's Downtown East Side on Hastings Street. When I met him, he had been clean from drugs and alcohol for 12 years. Brian was running a recovery house in Surrey, and as a part of the treatment, a certified counselor would come into work with the residents. To this story, I will refer to him as Ray.

Over three years I came to know Ray quite well along with his girlfriend Kate. I also engaged in private sessions with Ray.

Have you ever had a premonition that something is going to happen? You see it in frames as if you are actually watching it happen in real time. It's vivid, a strong, detailed, and intuitive vision. Clear and intense vision of the future, I did, and I live every day with deep regret that I didn't believe and act on what I saw because I didn't trust in it, a gift that I will never take for granted. One day, I had a vision that was clear as day; my vision was Kate being chased into a house by a man. She tried to hide under a desk in a living room to no avail. In my vision, I could not see the man's face. I didn't know who it was. I saw him raise the gun and shoot Kate.

In my premonition the next day, I was sitting in my car in the Recovery House driveway waiting for Brian to come out when Ray came out to tell us that Kate was shot by her ex-husband.

A few days later, I was, in fact, sitting in my car in the driveway at the Recovery House waiting for Brian when Ray and Brian came out to the car and told me that Kate had been shot by her ex-husband. He explained how it happened in detail, and it was exactly what I had envisioned. Right down to the layout of the living room and Kate trying to hide under the desk.

I was devastated that I had the premonition and didn't act on it. Grateful that Kate survived!

In my mind, it was just a horrible nightmare or day terror, and why would I visualize something like that? Sometimes, you have to trust your gut and hope that if you choose to act on it that people don't think that you are crazy. I was and always am harder on myself than anyone else. Everyone, including Kate, was very supportive when I told them.

"I feel there are two people inside me – me and my intuition. If I go against her, she'll screw me every time, and if I follow her, we get along quite nicely."
Kim Basinger

PART 2

WOMEN LIKE ME
MOVEMENT

"You must train your intuition – you must trust the small voice inside you which tells you exactly what to say, what to decide."
Ingrid Bergman

14

DO YOU BELIEVE IN YOUR DREAMS?

During the spring of 2016, I questioned my life's purpose.

Despite a successful sales, marketing, and promotions career span-ning over three decades, I had lost sight of my passion. Over the previous years, I had assisted more than three thousand satisfied clients, yet something was missing. I knew it was time for a change, but what direction should I take?

One evening, as I slept, I was awoken by a profoundly transformative vision in the form of a dream.

I recall being taken from where I was and led back. There was a bright light, and I said, "I don't want to go back; I want to stay here with you." I was told, "No, you have to go back; you're not finished yet."

I felt highly stressed and unhappy as I longed to remain where I was at that moment.

"But I don't know my purpose," I said. Someone responded, "You are your purpose." I recall experiencing anxiety and saying, "But I don't know what to do."

As I opened my eyes, a single word entered my mind: "Write!" Suddenly, I was fully awake.

Welcome to Women Like Me.

Julie Fairhurst, Founder of Women Like Me

"Trust yourself. You know more than you think you do."
Benjamin Spock

15

A COMMUNITY OF WOMEN LIKE ME

If you do not already belong to the Women Like Me community, I encourage you to consider joining. It is a great place to find support and connect with other women. You can also participate in discussions, ask questions, and share resources.

Joining the Women Like Me Community is a great way to connect with women with similar experiences and learn from their successes and challenges. It can also be a fantastic way to find mentors and role models. So, if you are a woman looking for support, please consider joining the Women Like Me Community. You will not regret it!

The Women Like Me Community is a social network connecting women with similar interests, goals, and concerns. Whether you are a working professional or working at home and a stay-at-home mom, this community is for you.

The Women Like Me Community - Julie Fairhurst is a Facebook group of like-minded women who want to pay it forward and lift others to promote healing in the world. They believe that by doing this, they can help to create a world that is kinder and more compassionate.

The Women Like Me Community - Julie Fairhurst is a place where you can feel safe and supported. It is a place where you can be yourself and share your story. It is a place where you can find encouragement, inspiration, and connection.

Throughout the year, the community writes community books, such as the one you are reading now. All community members are encouraged to participate in the writing of the books. There is no cost to any of the writers who wish to share their wisdom in the community books. If you have always dreamed of being a published author, this is a wonderful community to start fulfilling your dream.

If you have been looking for a community where you can belong, this is it.

Don't wait, join today!

Women Like Me Community – Julie Fairhurst https://www.facebook.com/groups/879482909307802

"It turns out that our intuition is a greater genius than we are."
Jim Shepard

16

WOMEN LIKE ME BOOK SERIES

Everyone has a story. And oftentimes, those stories can be powerful things that help us learn and grow. But for some people, their stories can be a source of pain. They may feel like they can't escape their past or that their story is holding them back from living their best lives.

If you're one of those people, know that you're not alone. And more importantly, know that there is hope. There are ways to turn your personal story into something positive and to find healing from the past.

One way is to share your story with others. This can be incredibly cathartic, and it can also help others who have been through similar experiences. You process your feelings and work through any trauma you may be carrying around.

And finally, don't forget that your story doesn't define you. You are more than your history. You are more than your pain. You are more than your mistakes. You are more than your story. You are strong, you are brave, and you are enough. So don't let your story hold you back.

Writing about your past can be very beneficial, both emotionally and psychologically. You can increase your feelings of well-being and even improve your physical health. When you write about your past experiences, you relive them in your mind. This can help you to process difficult or traumatic events, and it can also provide you with some closure.

Additionally, writing about your past can help you to understand yourself better and work through any unresolved issues. It can also allow you to see yourself in a new light, which can be both healing and empowering. In addition to helping you emotionally, writing about your past can also be beneficial physically.

Studies have shown that expressive writing can help to reduce stress, anxiety, and depression. It can also help to improve your immune system function and promote a sense of calm. So, if you're feeling stressed out or overwhelmed, consider picking up a pen and starting to write.

We only have one shot at this life, and it's our only shot. There are no do-overs. There are no second chances. So, we better make the most of it. We only have this moment right here, right now, and it's the only moment that matters. We are only given so much time on this planet, and we must spend it wisely. We only have so much energy and want to spend it on things that bring us joy. We only have so much love to give and want to give it to people who appreciate it.

If you're a woman and have had life experiences, the world wants to hear from you. Visit my website at www.womelikemestories.com and get in touch. The world will be waiting.

A story is a powerful thing. It can draw you in, take you on a journey, and leave you with a lasting impression. That's why I love listening to other people's stories. Everyone has a story to tell, and I'm always eager to hear a new one.

I want to hear from you. You can reach me by visiting my website and letting me know you're ready to tell your story. The world is waiting to hear what you have to say. So what are you waiting for?

Get in touch today!

Women Like Me Stories https://womenlikemestories.com/tell-your-story/

"Cease trying to work everything out with your minds. It will get you nowhere. Live by intuition and inspiration and let your whole life be a revelation."
Eileen Caddy

17

JULIE FAIRHURST

A prolific author, visionary publisher, and an
empowering writing coach helping women excel in life!

Julie Fairhurst is the Founder of the Women Like Me Book Program,
part of the Julie Fairhurst Academy. She started the Women Like Me
Project to help women tell their stories. Her unique storytelling
programs allow her clients to share their message with the world.
Julie has published 26 books to her credit and helped over 160
authors become published authors.

After spending 34 years as a sales, marketing, and promotional
expert, Julie now helps women entrepreneurs build their influence
and authority with their clients and customers to increase their
revenue and profits. A Master Persuader Julie is an expert at understanding human behavior and what triggers people to make a
purchase. She helps her clients develop marketing strategies that
appeal to their target audience and provides coaching on closing the
sale.

Julie is also a sought-after speaker, trainer, and prevention educator. She has delivered empowering workshops on safety issues to adolescents and adults and has presented to organizations such as the Vancouver Police Department, Justice Institute, University of British Columbia, Capilano College, Behavioral Society of British Columbia, Surrey Memorial Hospital, Teachers Association of North Vancouver, Shine Live, West Coast Woman's Show, Pink Stiletto Network, and more.

When Julie was young, her home life was chaotic and tumultuous. Her parents were constantly fighting, and she felt unsafe and unloved. As a result, she developed some bad habits and made poor decisions. As a teenager, she was headed down the wrong path, and it seemed like there was no hope for her.

But, somewhere deep inside, that little girl inside her showed up and reminded her that she wanted better for herself and her kids. Julie had no support from anyone, not a soul. She had to do it all on her own. She had no help from anyone, not a single person. She had to do everything by herself.

Many people say that you should never look back, but Julie does. Why? Because she wants to remember the journey that brought her to where she is today. And today, her life is very different.

Then, in 2019, Julie's beautiful 24-year-old niece died from a drug overdose on the streets of Vancouver, Canada. And that was the day she said enough! Her niece's death indirectly resulted from the generational beliefs and abuse that some of her siblings continue with their destructive lifestyles. So, when Julie says, "Enough is enough," she means it! Unfortunately, her story isn't unique.

When we don't face our issues, we pass on dysfunctional behaviors to future generations. This is what happened to her young niece. This is why she started the Women Like Me organization. When children grow up in toxic environments, they often develop behavioral issues that follow them into adulthood. This can lead to severe problems in their relationships, careers, and mental health. Julie's young niece was a victim of this.

Everyone has a story, and everyone's story matters. No matter what you've been through, you can improve your life. It's not always easy, but with determination and perseverance, anything is possible.

The first step is to believe in yourself. You have the power to create whatever future you want for yourself. The next step is to take action. You can't just sit and wait for good things to happen. You have to go out and make them happen.

And finally, you have to persevere. There will be setbacks, but that's no reason to give up. Keep going, and never give up on your dreams.

If you're willing to put in the work, you can change your life for the better. You have the power to do so. You have to believe in yourself and take steps to make it happen. So don't give up on yourself - you can do much more than you think. And when you're ready to start, Julie will be right here to help.

The
JULIE FAIRHURST
STORY

Healing Generations, One Story at a

JULIE FAIRHURST

"While the road has been anything but smooth, the decision to break free from the cycle of generational trauma has been the most empowering chapter of my story, a reminder that we are not bound by the circumstances of our birth but defined by the choices we make."

Julie Fairhurst

"There is a voice that doesn't use words. Listen."
Rumi

18

REACH OUT

Email:

julie@changeyourpath.ca

Women Like Me Stories:

www.womenlikemestories.com

YouTube:

Julie Fairhurst Women Like Me Stores and in Business:

https://www.youtube.com/channel/
UChFnLgiUC9mWnvp7jikKBw

Women Like Me on Facebook:

https://www.facebook.com/StoryCoachJulieFairhurst

Julie Fairhurst Academy on Facebook:

https://www.facebook.com/juliefairhurstcoaching

LinkedIn - Julie Fairhurst Certified Master Persuader:

https://www.linkedin.com/in/salesstrategistjuliefairhurst/

Instagram – Women Like Me Stories:

https://www.instagram.com/juliefairhurst_wlm_movement/

Facebook – Julie Fairhurst:

https://www.facebook.com/julie.fairhurst.7

"Notice what happens when you follow your intuitive feelings. The
result is usually increased energy and power,
and a sense of things flowing."
Shakti Gawain

READ MORE FROM JULIE FAIRHURST

& THE WOMEN LIKE ME AUTHORS

All books are available on Amazon or the Women Like Me Stories website. If you can't find the book you are looking for, reach out to me, and I can help. Or if you would like an autographed copy, please email at julie@changeyourpath.ca

Women Like Me Book Series

- Women Like Me – A Celebration of Courage and Triumphs
- Women Like Me – Stories of Resilience and Courage
- Women Like Me – A Tribute to the Brave and Wise
- Women Like Me – Breaking Through the Silence
- Women Like Me – From Loss to Living
- Women Like Me – Healing and Acceptance
- Women Like Me – Reclaiming Our Power
- Women Like Me – Whispers of Warriors: Women Who Refused to Stay Broken
- Women Like Me – Embracing the Unseen – The Courage to Surrender

- Women Like Me - Transforming Pain Into Wisdom and Love (Available late May 2024)

Women Like Me Community Book Series

- Women Like Me Community – Messages to My Younger Self
- Women Like Me Community – Sharing Words of Gratitude
- Women Like Me Community – Sharing What We Know to Be True
- Women Like Me Community – Journal for Self-Discovery
- Women Like Me Community – Sharing Life's Important Lessons
- Women Like Me Community – Having Better Relationships
- Women Like Me Community – Honoring the Women in Our Lives
- Women Like Me Community – Letters to Our Future Selves
- Women Like Me Community – The Warrior Within
- Women Like Me Community – Whisper's Within The Power of Women's Intuition

Women Like Me in Kenya

(100% of the profits go directly to these 26 Kenyan Authors. The Women Like Me Program covers all costs associated with producing and publishing the Kenya books)

- Women Like Me – Strong Women in Kenya
- Women Like Me – Through the Eyes of Kenyan Women
- Women Like Me – The Children of Kenya (Available June 2024)

Sales and Personal Growth

- The Julie Fairhurst Story – Healing Generations, One Story at a Time
- From Idea to Bestseller – Writing for Self-Help Authors
- Positivity Makes All the Difference
- Powerful Persuasion – Unlocking the Five Key Strategies for Business Success
- Transferring Enthusiasm - The Sales Book for Your Business Growth
- Agent Matchmaker: How to Find Your Real Estate Soulmate"
- Agent Etiquette – 14 Things You Didn't Learn in Real Estate School
- 7 Keys to Success – How to Become a Real Estate Badass
- 30 Days to Real Estate Action – Real Strategies & Real Connections
- Why Agents Quit the Business

"Listen to the wind, it talks. Listen to the silence, it speaks.
Listen to your heart, it knows."
Native American Proverb

www.ingramcontent.com/pod-product-compliance
Lightning Source LLC
Chambersburg PA
CBHW060808050426
42449CB00008B/1590